SPIDERS

Published by Creative Education, Inc., 123 South Broad Street, Mankato, Minnesota 56001

Printed by permission of Wildlife Education, Ltd.

Library of Congress Cataloging-in-Publication Data

Biel, Timothy L.
Spiders / by Timothy Levi Biel.
p.   cm. — (Zoobooks)
Originally published as an issue of Zoobooks: San Diego, CA: 1985.
Summary: Identifies different types of spiders, describing physical characteristics, habits, and habitats.
ISBN 0-88682-410-9
1. Spiders—Juvenile literature. [1. Spiders.] I. Title. II. Series: Zoo books (Mankato, Minn.)
QL452.2.B54   1991   595.4'4—dc20   91-9940 CIP AC

SPIDERS

Zoobook Series Created by
John Bonnett Wexo

Written by
Timothy Levi Biel

Zoological Consultant
Charles R. Schroeder, D.V.M.
Director Emeritus
San Diego Zoo &
San Diego Wild Animal Park

Scientific Consultants
Dr. Herbert W. Levi
Museum of Comparative Zoology,
Harvard University

Dr. Ron Monroe
Entomology Department,
San Diego State University

Creative Education

Art Credits

Main Art: Walter Stuart
Pages Eight and Nine: Walter Stuart; **Pages Ten and Eleven:** Walter Stuart; **Page Eleven: Bottom,** Jim Melli; **Pages Twelve and Thirteen:** Walter Stuart; **Page Twelve: Bottom,** Ed Abrams; **Pages Sixteen and Seventeen:** Walter Stuart; **Page Seventeen: Bottom,** Jim Melli; **Page Eighteen:** Jim Melli; **Page Nineteen:** Walter Stuart; **Page Twenty-Two:** Walter Stuart; **Inside Back Cover:** Jim Melli.

Photographic Credits

Cover: James P. Rowan (Click Chicago); **Pages Six and Seven:** Adolf Schmidecker (Alpha/FPG); **Page Nine: Top,** William Ferguson; **Middle,** M.P.C. Fogden (Bruce Coleman, Ltd.); **Bottom,** Hans Pfletschinger (Peter Arnold Inc.); **Page Ten:** Hans Pfletschinger (Peter Arnold Inc.); **Page Eleven: Top,** Frieder Saver (Bruce Coleman Ltd.); **Bottom,** James P. Rowan (Click Chicago); **Page Twelve:** Richard Walters; **Page Thirteen:** Hans Pfletschinger (Peter Arnold Inc.); **Pages Fourteen and Fifteen:** Michael Fogden (Animals Animals); **Page Sixteen:** Richard K. La Val (Animals Animals); **Page Seventeen: Top,** Stephen Dalton (Natural History Photos); **Middle,** Jane Burton (Bruce Coleman Inc.); **Bottom,** Alan Blank (Bruce Coleman Inc.); **Page Eighteen: Top,** Robert Mitchell, **Middle,** Hans Pfletschinger (Peter Arnold Inc.); **Bottom,** Rod Planck (Tom Stack & Assoc.); **Page Nineteen: Top,** Kerry T. Givens; **Page Twenty:** William Ferguson; **Page Twenty-One: Bottom,** J. Serrao; **Inside Back Cover: Top,** Richard Walters; **Bottom,** J.A. Grant (Natural Science Photos).

Our Thanks To: Mr. Saul Frommer (University of California at Riverside); Michael Kassem; Mike Mitchell, Andy Natonabah, Peggy Scott (Navajo Community College); David Faulkner (San Diego Museum of Natural History); Melanie Biel; Richard Leonhardt; Tom Clark; Pamela Stuart.

Contents

Spiders are not going to win any popularity contests. When people see spiders, they react in different ways. Some people just scream and run away. Others try to kill every spider they see. Gardeners may get out the poison and kill even the spiders they can't see. Occasionally, however, a person will just stop and watch with fascination as a spider spins its web.

Of all possible reactions, this is probably the wisest, because spiders rarely do anything to harm us. Out of thousands of different spiders in the world, only a handful are poisonous to people. The most common poisonous spiders, such as the *Black Widow* and the *Brown Recluse* (WRECK-LOOSE) rarely bite people. In fact, far more people die each year from bee and wasp stings than from spider bites.

Most spiders are actually very helpful. They do not harm plants, as some people think. Instead, they protect plants by controlling insects. Spiders are the most important predators of insects in the world. So if you see spiders in a garden, it does not mean the garden is unhealthy. It just means the spiders are helping it stay healthy.

If you take the time to watch spiders, you may be surprised by what you see. There are many wonderful colors, shapes, and sizes of spiders. Some spin beautiful webs. They may perform daring acrobatic feats on their silk-thin threads. Other spiders spin no webs at all. They stalk insects on the ground with all the skill and ferocity of a tiger hunting big game.

Scientists have named about 30 thousand species of spiders. But they think this is only one-fourth of all the different spiders in the world. In most species, you can easily tell the female spider from the male, because the females are much larger. For example, the female Black Widow weighs about *one hundred times* as much as the male.

Female spiders lay eggs. And the baby spiders that hatch from these eggs are called *spiderlings*. After hatching, most spiders live less than a full year, but there are some remarkable exceptions. Tarantulas do not become mature adults until they are 10 or 11 years old. And female tarantulas often live another 10 years after that!

What is a spider? Many people probably *think* they know, but they may not be able to tell a spider from other small creatures. Can you? Do you know how many legs spiders have? Do they have wings like an insect, or a stinger like a scorpion?

Like insects, spiders are *arthropods* (ARE-THROW-PODS). This means they have legs with many joints, and a hard skeleton that covers the outside of their body. But look closely at the pictures on these pages, and you will see how spiders are different from insects and other arthropods, like scorpions and mites. And in the box at right, you will see the body parts that all spiders have.

A spider's body has two main parts. The "front" part is called the *cephalothorax* (sef-uh-low-THOR-ax). This is where the spider has its eyes, mouth, and stomach. All spiders have 8 legs, and they are also attached to this part of the body.

CEPHALOTHORAX

FANGS

JAWS

PEDIPALPS

8 LEGS

The spider's mouth has two large *jaws*. At the tip of each jaw is a sharp, curved *fang*. And alongside each jaw is a *pedipalp* (PED-uh-palp). Pedipalps are like "feelers" that the spider uses to sense what is around it. They can also be used to hold prey down while the spider bites it with its fangs.

JUMPING SPIDER

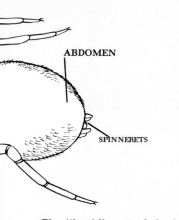

ABDOMEN

SPINNERETS

The "back" part of the body is called the *abdomen*. Silk is produced inside the abdomen, and it is spun out through *spinnerets* (SPIN-ur-ets) that are located at the end of the abdomen.

IS THIS A SPIDER?

The Crane Fly has long legs like a spider. But count them. It only has 6 legs. That's because Crane Flies are insects, not spiders. You can also tell that this is not a spider because it has wings. And spiders do *not* have wings.

SCORPION

IS THIS A SPIDER?

Mites are so tiny they look like walking specks of dust. But magnified, like the Velvet Mite below, they look like spiders. In fact, they are very closely related. If you look carefully, however, you will see that the mite's body is not divided into two parts the way a spider's is. Instead, it is all one piece with no separation between the head and abdomen.

IS THIS A SPIDER?

Scorpions have 8 legs and a pair of pedipalps, just like spiders. But did you notice that a scorpion's pedipalps are huge pincers? And that its long thin body is divided into several segments? Also, the scorpion's "tail end" has a stinger. All these things make scorpions different from spiders.

VELVET MITE

9

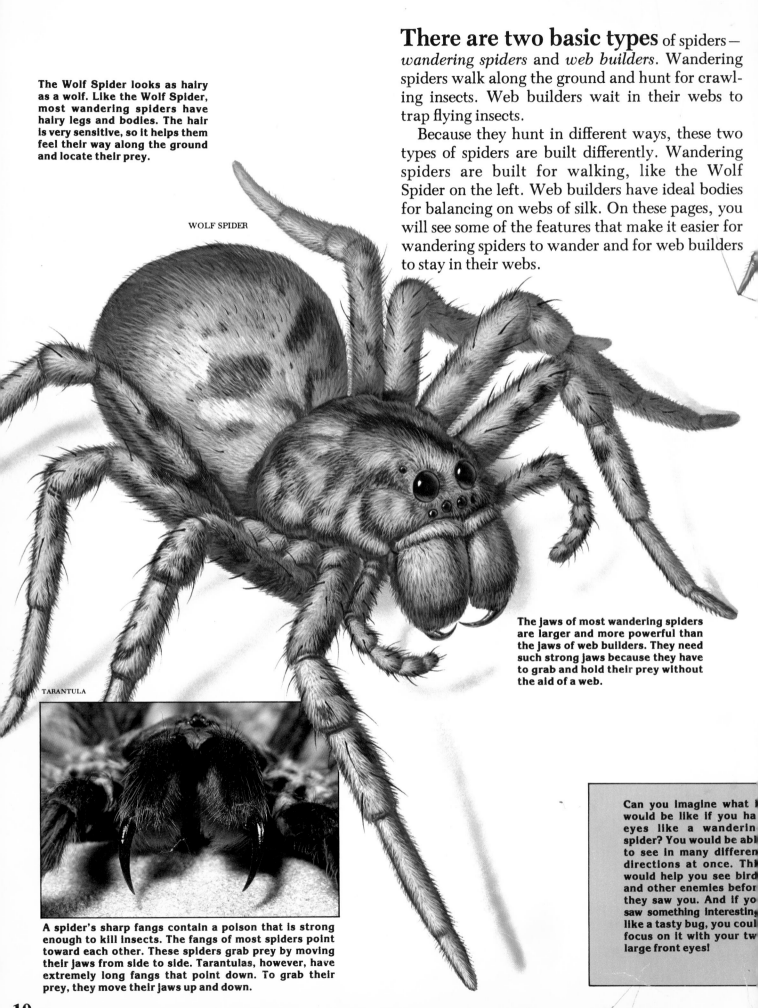

The Wolf Spider looks as hairy as a wolf. Like the Wolf Spider, most wandering spiders have hairy legs and bodies. The hair is very sensitive, so it helps them feel their way along the ground and locate their prey.

WOLF SPIDER

There are two basic types of spiders — *wandering spiders* and *web builders*. Wandering spiders walk along the ground and hunt for crawling insects. Web builders wait in their webs to trap flying insects.

Because they hunt in different ways, these two types of spiders are built differently. Wandering spiders are built for walking, like the Wolf Spider on the left. Web builders have ideal bodies for balancing on webs of silk. On these pages, you will see some of the features that make it easier for wandering spiders to wander and for web builders to stay in their webs.

The jaws of most wandering spiders are larger and more powerful than the jaws of web builders. They need such strong jaws because they have to grab and hold their prey without the aid of a web.

TARANTULA

A spider's sharp fangs contain a poison that is strong enough to kill insects. The fangs of most spiders point toward each other. These spiders grab prey by moving their jaws from side to side. Tarantulas, however, have extremely long fangs that point down. To grab their prey, they move their jaws up and down.

Can you imagine what it would be like if you had eyes like a wandering spider? You would be able to see in many different directions at once. This would help you see birds and other enemies before they saw you. And if you saw something interesting, like a tasty bug, you could focus on it with your two large front eyes!

10

Web builders use their long skinny legs to perform daring "high wire acts." With 8 long legs to help them balance, they seem to dance and glide over their webs.

RED WIDOW

Although all spiders can spin silk, the real experts are the web builders. They usually have 3 or 4 pairs of spinnerets that spin different textures of silk to do different jobs.

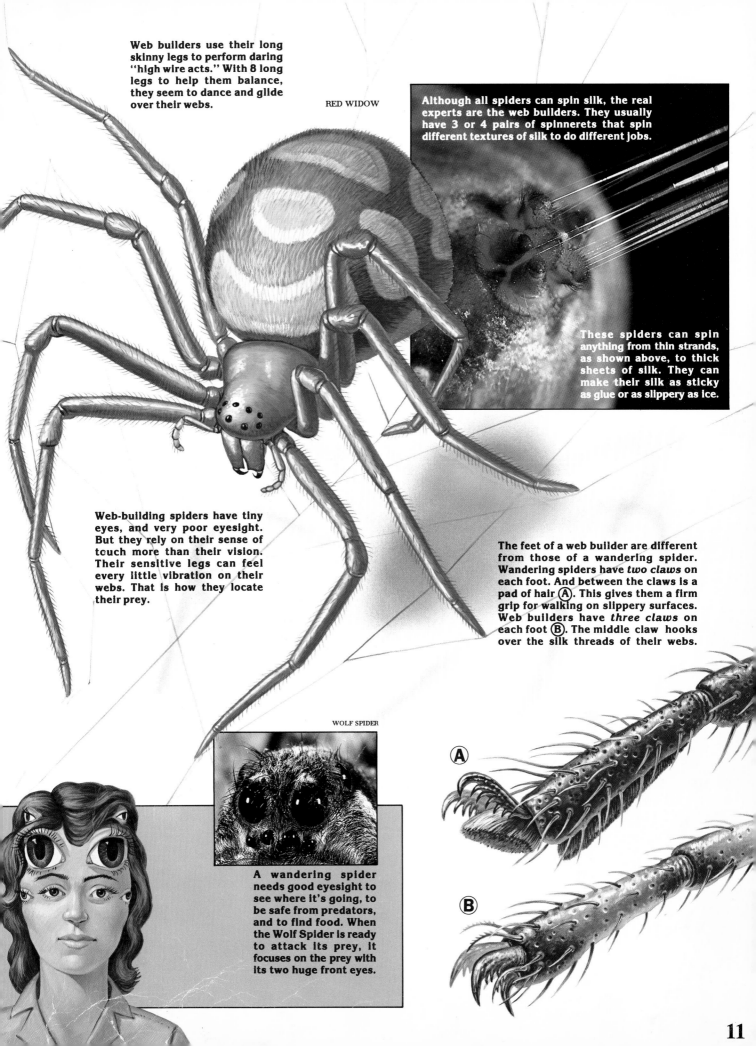

These spiders can spin anything from thin strands, as shown above, to thick sheets of silk. They can make their silk as sticky as glue or as slippery as ice.

Web-building spiders have tiny eyes, and very poor eyesight. But they rely on their sense of touch more than their vision. Their sensitive legs can feel every little vibration on their webs. That is how they locate their prey.

The feet of a web builder are different from those of a wandering spider. Wandering spiders have *two claws* on each foot. And between the claws is a pad of hair Ⓐ. This gives them a firm grip for walking on slippery surfaces. Web builders have *three claws* on each foot Ⓑ. The middle claw hooks over the silk threads of their webs.

WOLF SPIDER

Ⓐ

A wandering spider needs good eyesight to see where it's going, to be safe from predators, and to find food. When the Wolf Spider is ready to attack its prey, it focuses on the prey with its two huge front eyes.

Ⓑ

11

Web-building spiders use silk to build shelters, catch prey, and move from place to place. For these things, a spider must have different kinds of silk. Fortunately, most spiders can make their silk thick or thin, weak or strong, slippery or sticky, or just about any way they need it.

There are many different kinds of web-building spiders. And they build different kinds of webs. Some webs look very beautiful while others just look like a tangle of threads. But every web is just right for its builder. You can even tell by the shape of the web what kind of spider built it. Can you find an *Orb Weaver*, a *Triangle Spider*, a *Funnel Weaver*, a *Cobweb Weaver*, a *"Net Thrower,"* and a *Water Spider* on these pages by looking at their webs?

Most web builders wrap their prey with sticky silk before they bite it. This prevents the prey from kicking its way free, or from stinging to defend itself. Also, once its food is wrapped, the spider doesn't have to eat it until it gets hungry.

AN ORB WEAVER builds a web shaped like an *orb*, or circle. Day or night, its web is almost invisible. Some orb weavers sit in the center of their webs and wait for insects to fly into them. Others, like the Shamrock Spider at right, hide alongside the web until they feel it vibrating. Then they know they have caught something, so they rush out to attack it.

FUNNEL WEAVER

A FUNNEL WEAVER builds a web in the grass that is shaped like a funnel. This spider hides in the small end of the funnel, where it waits for insects to land on its web. Then it rushes out from its hiding place and grabs them.

Purse Web Spiders make *tubes* for webs and build them alongside tree trunks. They mix dirt with their silk to make the tube look like part of the tree. Then they spend most of their lives inside the tube waiting for insects to come by, like the grasshopper at right ①.

① ②

Some spiders use their silk in unusual ways. For example, the Bolas Spider makes a remarkable weapon by spinning a ball of sticky silk on the end of a strong thread. This spider attracts male moths by imitating the smell of a female moth. When the moth approaches, the spider hits it with its gooey ball of silk. The moth sticks to the ball, and the spider pulls in its line.

In a flash, the spider thrusts its fangs through the silk wall of the tube. Then it grabs its prey and pulls it inside ②.

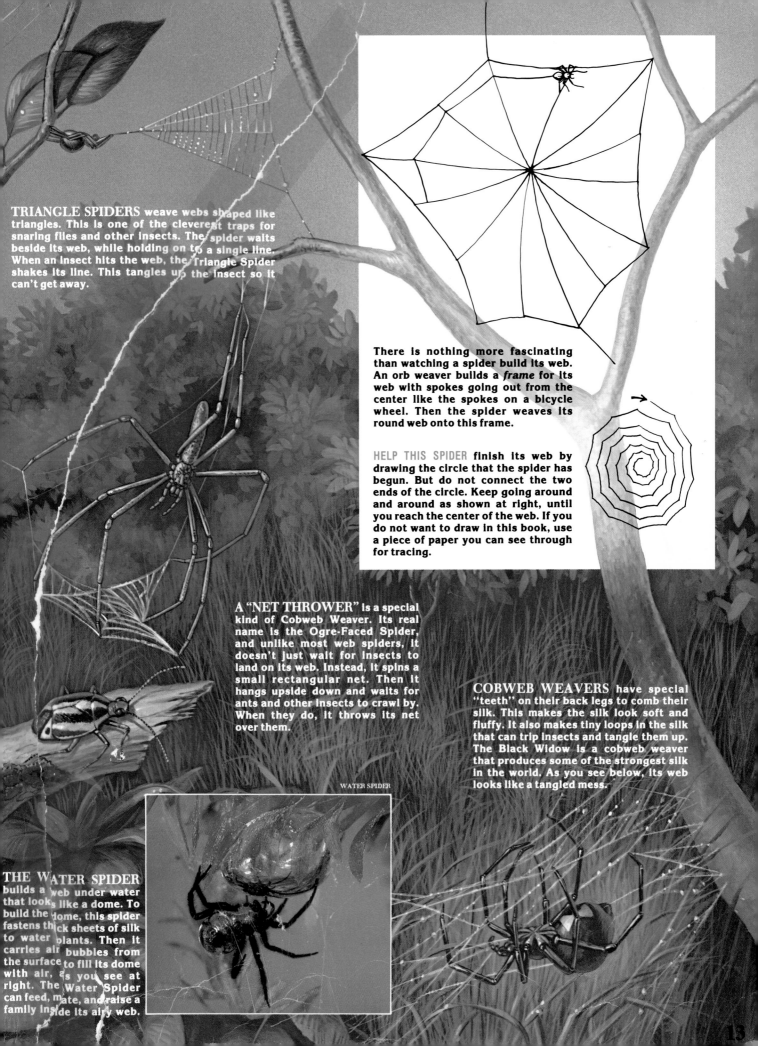

TRIANGLE SPIDERS weave webs shaped like triangles. This is one of the cleverest traps for snaring flies and other insects. The spider waits beside its web, while holding on to a single line. When an insect hits the web, the Triangle Spider shakes its line. This tangles up the insect so it can't get away.

There is nothing more fascinating than watching a spider build its web. An orb weaver builds a *frame* for its web with spokes going out from the center like the spokes on a bicycle wheel. Then the spider weaves its round web onto this frame.

HELP THIS SPIDER finish its web by drawing the circle that the spider has begun. But do not connect the two ends of the circle. Keep going around and around as shown at right, until you reach the center of the web. If you do not want to draw in this book, use a piece of paper you can see through for tracing.

A "NET THROWER" is a special kind of Cobweb Weaver. Its real name is the Ogre-Faced Spider, and unlike most web spiders, it doesn't just wait for insects to land on its web. Instead, it spins a small rectangular net. Then it hangs upside down and waits for ants and other insects to crawl by. When they do, it throws its net over them.

COBWEB WEAVERS have special "teeth" on their back legs to comb their silk. This makes the silk look soft and fluffy. It also makes tiny loops in the silk that can trip insects and tangle them up. The Black Widow is a cobweb weaver that produces some of the strongest silk in the world. As you see below, its web looks like a tangled mess.

WATER SPIDER

THE WATER SPIDER builds a web under water that looks like a dome. To build the dome, this spider fastens thick sheets of silk to water plants. Then it carries air bubbles from the surface to fill its dome with air, as you see at right. The Water Spider can feed, mate, and raise a family inside its airy web.

15

WANDERING SPIDER

15

Wandering spiders do not build webs. They live on the ground, in burrows, under rocks, inside tree hollows, and in other protected places. Most of them are active hunters, because they cannot just sit and wait for prey to come to them. Instead, wandering spiders must go looking for food.

There are many different kinds of wandering spiders, and they hunt in different ways. Many are like tigers that stalk prey along the ground before leaping on them. Some climb trees, and others dig burrows to hide from their prey. There are spiders that "fish" for prey, and there is even one that catches insects by *spitting* on them! Insects are the main food of all these spiders, but you may be surprised to see the other things that some of them can catch.

TARANTULA

Some tarantulas can capture small tree frogs because they are good at climbing trees. They have pads of sticky hair on the bottoms of their feet that help them climb on slippery leaves and branches.

16

Most spiders are afraid of birds, but the Bird-eating spiders of South America aren't. These tarantulas may get as big as hummingbirds. Sometimes they even try to sneak up on hummingbirds and drag them from their nests! However, if a hummingbird sees one of these spiders coming, it usually flies away before the spider can catch it.

To catch prey, Jumping Spiders often leap more than *50 times* their body length. If you could jump as well as a jumping spider, you could leap from one end of a football field to the other in a single bound!

JUMPING SPIDER

Jumping Spiders not only jump a long way, they also jump very accurately. They usually stalk an insect until they are about a foot away from it (30 centimeters). Then they take a giant leap and land right on their prey.

FISHING SPIDER

This wandering spider goes fishing for most of its food. It can run across the surface of the water and grab insects that have landed or fallen on the water. It can also dive beneath the surface to catch water bugs and even small fish, as you see above.

TRAPDOOR SPIDER

The Spitting Spider traps insects by spitting on them! It spits a sticky glue from its fangs. This keeps the prey stuck to the ground so it cannot run away.

A Trapdoor Spider *looks* like a wandering spider, but it doesn't wander. Instead, it hides in a burrow to ambush prey. This spider lines its burrow with silk and covers it with a "trapdoor." Inside, the spider waits until it feels the vibration of an insect passing by. Then it pops out and captures it.

Baby spiders grow up quickly. In fact, the entire life of a spider may be less than one year long. Many spiderlings hatch in the spring from eggs laid the summer before. Others hatch in the fall and live through the winter.

For the first few days of life, most spiderlings live with other newly hatched spiders. But before long, every spider must begin to look for food. In order to spread out and find places to hunt or build their webs, young spiders have a special way of traveling through the air, called *ballooning*.

Only a small number of ballooning spiders land safely and find enough food to survive. But if they do, they usually become adults by late summer. Then they are ready to mate. Shortly after mating, most male spiders die. But females live longer, so they can lay their eggs. Some mother spiders even live long enough to guard their eggs and protect the young after they hatch. One typical spider that does this is the Wolf Spider, shown below.

After a few days, the spiderlings are big enough to climb out of the egg sac. In some species, these newly hatched spiders work together to build a web. This is called a *nursery web* Ⓒ. The young spiders stay on the nursery web until they get hungry. Then they set out to find a place of their own.

When it first hatches, the spiderling remains in the egg sac. Its tiny body is not completely formed. And it cannot see or move Ⓑ.

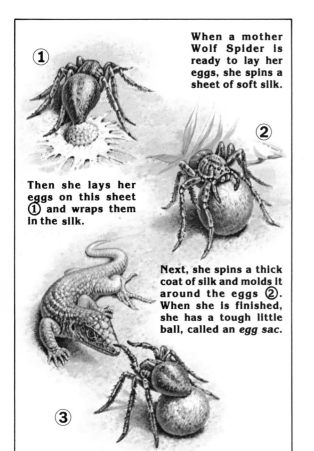

① When a mother Wolf Spider is ready to lay her eggs, she spins a sheet of soft silk.

Then she lays her eggs on this sheet ① and wraps them in the silk.

② Next, she spins a thick coat of silk and molds it around the eggs ②. When she is finished, she has a tough little ball, called an *egg sac.*

③ The mother keeps her egg sac close to her. She guards it from lizards and other small predators ③.

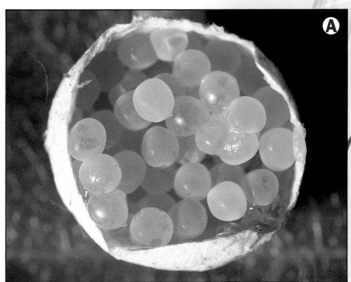

Spiders begin life as tiny eggs in an egg sac. The number of eggs varies from species to species. But often there are more than a hundred eggs in a single egg sac Ⓐ.

FEMALE WOLF SPIDER AND YOUNG

④ After her babies hatch, a mother Wolf Spider has an unusual way of looking after them. She carries them on her back wherever she goes. For several days, she may carry hundreds of little spiderlings this way ④.

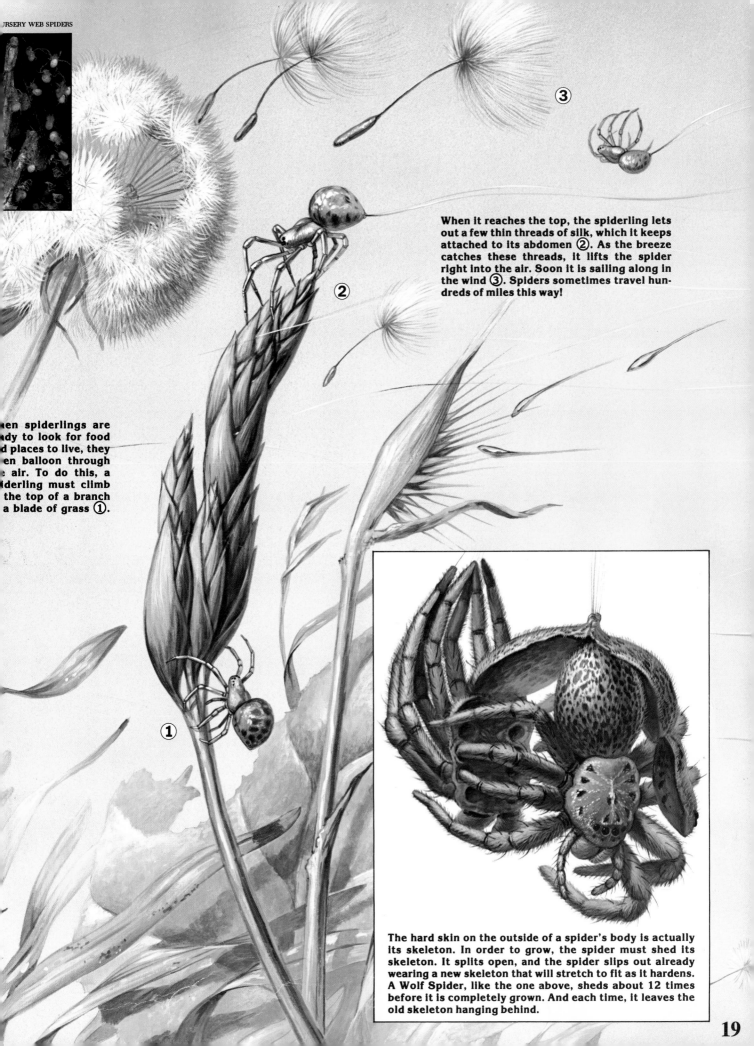

③

② When it reaches the top, the spiderling lets out a few thin threads of silk, which it keeps attached to its abdomen ②. As the breeze catches these threads, it lifts the spider right into the air. Soon it is sailing along in the wind ③. Spiders sometimes travel hundreds of miles this way!

When spiderlings are ready to look for food and places to live, they often balloon through the air. To do this, a spiderling must climb to the top of a branch or a blade of grass ①.

①

The hard skin on the outside of a spider's body is actually its skeleton. In order to grow, the spider must shed its skeleton. It splits open, and the spider slips out already wearing a new skeleton that will stretch to fit as it hardens. A Wolf Spider, like the one above, sheds about 12 times before it is completely grown. And each time, it leaves the old skeleton hanging behind.

There are many strange and beautiful spiders in the world. One of the strangest is this tropical orb weaver. The thorny shield that covers its abdomen discourages birds and other predators from eating it.

Crab Spiders hide in flowers and ambush insects. Some of them even change colors so they can hide better. The Crab Spider above happens to be yellow, because it is sitting on a yellow flower. But if it were on a white flower, this spider would turn white!

The ancient Greeks believed that a woman named *Arachne* (a-RACK-knee) was the ancestor of all spiders. This is where the word *arachnid* comes from, which is the name scientists sometimes use for spiders. Arachne's story was often told in pictures such as this.

Arachne was a weaver. And her weavings were the most beautiful in all of Greece. But Arachne had one fault—she was very proud. She even claimed that she could weave better than the Greek goddess Athena (a-THEE-na). This made the goddess so angry that she turned Arachne into a tiny spider. And the cloth that Arachne was weaving became her web.

People have mixed feelings about spiders. On the one hand, they are often afraid of spiders. But on the other hand, they are fascinated by them. People usually fear spiders because they do not know much about them. And as they learn more about spiders, they become more fascinated by them, and less frightened.

In ancient times, people overcame their fear of spiders by creating myths and legends about them. Today, we still enjoy telling these old tales. But we can overcome our fear of spiders by learning about them. And if we follow a few safety rules, we can learn a lot about spiders just by watching them in our yards, parks, and playgrounds.

Ⓐ People may have learned to weave by watching spiders. At least that is what the Navaho Indians once believed. According to an ancient Navaho legend, a young girl wandered away from her village one day. The girl found a big hole in the ground, and she peeked inside.

Ⓑ To her great surprise the young girl had discovered the underground home of the Spider Woman, who was sitting at her loom weaving a beautiful blanket. The Spider Woman welcomed the girl, who stayed with her for several days and learned the secrets of weaving. When the girl returned to her people, she taught them everything the Spider Woman had shown her. And to this day, the Navahos are known for their beautifully woven blankets, like the one at left.

BROWN RECLUSE

Only a few species of spiders are poisonous to humans. But for your own safety, you should learn to recognize such common poisonous spiders as the Black Widow (below) and the Brown Recluse (right). The Brown Recluse is common in the southern and western United States. It is brown, it has 6 eyes, and it has a mark on its back that looks like a violin. Can you find the violin?

BLACK WIDOW

Black Widows are common throughout the United States and southern Canada. They are shiny and black, with a round abdomen that looks like a marble. On the underside of the abdomen, Black Widows have a red mark that is shaped like an hourglass. Can you find the hourglass?

Spiders do not go looking for people to bite. In fact, they try to stay out of people's way. But you may find them in unswept corners of houses, barns, and garages, because these are good places to build webs. If you sweep the corners regularly, spiders will not stay there.

TO BE SAFE, always follow the rules below.

RULE 1: Do not touch a spider if you aren't sure what kind it is.

RULE 2: If you happen to get bitten by a spider, catch it with a jar, so it can be identified if necessary.

You can learn about spiders by watching them. And you can find them just about anywhere. If you search for them, you may find web-building spiders repairing their webs or making new ones. You may see them catching or tying up insects. Look beside rocks, and you may find Wolf Spiders and Jumping Spiders hunting for prey.

If you keep an eye on the same web for several days, you will see some interesting changes. Some day, you may see two spiders on the same web—a big female and a much smaller male. A few days later, you could see a female carrying her egg sac fastened to her abdomen. And one day, you may even find a webful of baby spiders.

You can collect spider webs without harming spiders. To do this, you need a can of spray lacquer, a pair of scissors, and a supply of sturdy black paper.

First, spray the web with 3 or 4 *light coats of lacquer* ①. When the lacquer dries, place a piece of paper behind the web. Then cut it free and catch it on your paper ②. Spray the web with a final coat of lacquer so it will stick to the paper ③.

Index